D1408650

REFLECTIONS
ON
MADISON COUNTY

A Photographic Journey
Mark F. Heffron

Mitchell Beazley

Dedicated to Jayne, John, and Hannah

Conception and Photography: Mark F. Heffron
Editorial direction and design: Gary Chassman
Art direction: Dana Jinkins
Production: Randi Jinkins
Associate Editor: Jill Bobrow

Photographs on pages 5 and 79 © Cindy Kilgore Brown
Photographs on pages 50 and 77 © Dana Jinkins

First published in Great Britain in 1994
by Mitchell Beazley
an imprint of Reed Consumer Books Limited
Michelin House, 81 Fulham Road
London SW3 6RB
and Auckland, Melbourne, Singapore and Toronto

Created and Produced by Ex Press Bridges Publishing Inc.
P.O. Box 1066
Waitsfield, Vermont 05673

Printed in Italy
First Edition
10 9 8 7 6 5 4 3 2 1

A CIP Catalogue record for this book is available
from the British Library
ISBN 1 - 85732 - 544 - 3

*Reflections on Madison County: A Photographic
Journey* is not sponsored by, affiliated, connected
or associated with Robert James Waller or any
publication of Warner Books, Inc., Time Warner Inc.

All photographs with the exception of pages
5, 79, 50, and 77 © Mark F. Heffron

Poetry by Rainer Maria Rilke, edited and translated
by Robert Bly from *Selected Poems of Rainer Maria
Rilke* and poems by Rachel Carson from *The Sense of
Wonder*, reprinted with the kind permission of
HarperCollins Publishers Inc. New York

Selections from the *Poems of W.B.Yeats: A New
Edition*, Edited by Richard Finneran. Copyright 1919,
1933, 1934, by Macmillan Publishing Company,
Copyright renewed 1947, 1961, 1962 by Bertha
Georgie Yeats. Reprinted with permission from
Macmillan Publishing Company.

Excerpts from *The Wilderness World of John Muir*
edited by Edwin Way Teale. Copyright 1954 by
Edwin W. Teale, © renewed 1982 by Nellie D. Teale.
Reprinted by permission of Houghton Mifflin
Company. All rights reserved.

Aldo Leopold is quoted from his book
A Sand County Almanac, with other essays on
conservation from *Round River* by Aldo Leopold.
Copyright © 1949, 1953, 1966, renewed 1977, 1981
by Oxford University Press, Inc. Reprinted by
permission of Oxford University Press.

Why meet we on the bridge of time to change one greeting and to part?

Sir Richard Burton

I live my life in growing orbits
which move out over the things of the world.
Perhaps I can never achieve the last,
but that will be my attempt.

I am circling around God, around the ancient tower,
and I have been circling for a thousand years,
and I still don't know if I am a falcon, or a storm,
or a great song.

Rainer Maria Rilke

Those who contemplate the beauty of the earth find reserves of strength that will endure as long as life lasts. There is symbolic as well as actual beauty in the migration of the birds, the ebb and flow of the tides, the folded bud ready for the spring. There is something infinitely healing in the repeated refrains of nature—the assurance that dawn comes after night, and spring after the winter.

Rachel Carson

Only by going alone in silence, can one truly get into the heart of the wilderness. All other travel is mere dust and hotels and baggage and chatter.

John Muir

There is a love of wild nature in everybody,
an ancient mother-love ever showing itself
whether recognized or no, and however
covered by cares and duties.

John Muir

The leaves are falling, falling as if from far up,
as if orchards were dying high in space.
Each leaf falls as if it were motioning "no."

And tonight the heavy earth is falling
away from all the other stars in the loneliness.

Rainer Maria Rilke

My eyes already touch the sunny hill,
going far ahead of the road I have begun.
So we are grasped by what we cannot grasp;
it has its inner light, even from a distance—

and changes us, even if we do not reach it,
into something else, which, hardly sensing it, we already are;
a gesture waves us on, answering our own wave . . .
but what we feel is the wind in our faces.

Rainer Maria Rilke

Weave a circle round him thrice,
    And close your eyes with holy dread,
    For he on honey-dew hath fed,
And drunk the milk of Paradise.

Samuel Taylor Coleridge

She sings as the moon sings:
'I am I, am I;
The greater grows my light
The further that I fly.'
All creation shivers
With that sweet cry.

W.B. Yeats

Everything that man esteems
Endures a moment or a day.
Love's pleasure drives his love away,
The painter's brush consumes his dreams.

W.B. Yeats

Even memory is not necessary for love.
There is a land of the living and a land of the
dead and the bridge is love, the only survival,
the only meaning.

Thornton Wilder, The Bridge of San Luis Rey

I've spent my life making blunders. The advantage of growing old is that you become aware of your mistakes more quickly.

Pierre-Auguste Renoir

The Impressionist sees light as bathing everything. He sees the real living lines in a thousand irregular strokes, which, at a distance, establish life.

Jules Laforgue

We are poor passing facts,
warned by that to give
each figure in the photograph
his living name.

Robert Lowell

We live in time so little time
And we learn all so painfully,
That we may spare this hour's term
To practice for eternity.

Robert Penn Warren

We abuse land because we regard it as a commodity belonging to us. When we see land as a community to which we belong, we may begin to use it with love and respect.

Aldo Leopold, *A Sand County Almanac*

The Impressionist sees and renders nature as it is—that is, wholly in the vibration of color.

Jules Laforgue

To be an artist you must learn to know the laws of nature.

Pierre-Auguste Renoir

Slowly the west reaches for clothes of new colors
which it passes to a row of ancient trees.
You look, and soon these two worlds both leave you,
one part climbs toward heaven, one sinks to earth,

leaving you, not really belonging to either,
not so hopelessly dark as that house that is silent,
not so unswervingly given to the eternal as that thing
that turns to a star each night and climbs—

leaving you (it is impossible to untangle the threads)
your own life, timid and standing high and growing,
so that, sometimes blocked in, sometimes reaching out,
one moment your life is a stone in you, and the next, a star.

Rainer Maria Rilke

I whispered,"I am too young."
And then, "I am old enough";
Wherefore I threw a penny
To find out if I might love.
"Go and love, go and love, young man,
If the lady be young and fair."
Ah, penny, brown penny, brown penny,
I am looped in the loops of her hair.

O love is the crooked thing,
There is nobody wise enough
To find out all that is in it,
For he would be thinking of love
Till the stars had run away
And the shadows eaten the moon.
Ah, penny, brown penny, brown penny,
One cannot begin it too soon.

W.B. Yeats

Wine comes in at the mouth
And love comes in at the eye;
That's all we shall know for truth
Before we grow old and die.
I lift the glass to my mouth,
I look at you, and I sigh.

W.B. Yeats

This grand show is eternal. It is always
sunrise somewhere; the dew is never all
dried at once; a shower is forever falling;
vapor is ever rising. Eternal sunrise, eternal
sunset, eternal dawn and gloaming, on sea
and continents and islands, each in its turn,
as the round earth rolls.

John Muir

In a field by the river my love and I did stand,
And on my leaning shoulder she laid her snow-white hand.
She bid me take life easy, as the grass grows on the weirs;
but I was young and foolish, and now am full of tears.

W.B. Yeats

Why meet we on the bridge of Time
to change one greeting and to part?

Sir Richard Burton

What I like above all is serenity.

Pierre-Auguste Renoir

Wilderness is the raw material
out of which man has
hammered the artifact called
civilization.

Aldo Leopold

It was at the highest point in the arc of a bridge that I became aware suddenly of the depth and bitterness of my feelings about modern life, and of the profoundness of my yearning for a more vivid, simple, and peaceable world.

John Cheever, The Angel of the Bridge

In God's wildness lies the hope of the world—the great fresh, unblighted, unredeemed wilderness. The galling harness of civilization drops off, and the wounds heal ere we are aware.

John Muir

Most people are *on* the world, not in it—have
no conscious sympathy or relationship to
anything about them—undiffused, separate,
and rigidly alone like marbles of polished
stone, touching but separate.

John Muir

Shy one, shy one,
Shy one of my heart,
She moves in the firelight
Pensively apart.

She carries in the dishes,
And lays them in a row.
To an isle in the water
With her would I go.

She carries in the candles,
And lights the curtained room,
Shy in the doorway
And shy in the gloom;

And shy as a rabbit,
Helpful and shy.
To an isle in the water
With her would I fly.

W.B. Yeats

When the god, needing something, decided to become a swan,
he was astounded how lovely the bird was;
he was dizzy as he disappeared into the swan.
But his deceiving act soon pulled him into the doing,

before he had a chance to test all the new feelings
inside the being. And the woman, open to him,
recognized the One Soon To Be in the swan
and she knew: what he asked for

was something which, confused in her defending, she
could no longer keep from him. He pressed closer
and pushing his neck through her less and less firm hand

let the god loose into the darling woman.
Then for the first time he found his feathers marvelous
and lying in her soft place he became a swan.

Rainer Maria Rilke

Again, again, even if we know the country side of love,
and the tiny churchyard with its names mourning,
and the chasm, more and more silent, terrifying, into which
                                        the others
dropped: we walk out together anyway
beneath the ancient trees, we lie down again,
again, among the flowers, and face the sky.

Rainer Maria Rilke

For most of us, knowledge of our world comes largely through sight, yet we look about with such unseeing eyes that we are partially blind. One way to open your eyes to unnoticed beauty is to ask yourself,"What if I had never seen this before? What if I knew I would never see it again?"

Rachel Carson

I went out to the hazel wood,
Because a fire was in my head,
And cut and peeled a hazel wand,
And hooked a berry to a thread;
And when white moths were on the wing,
And moth-like stars were flickering out,
I dropped the berry in a stream
And caught a little silver trout.

When I had laid it on the floor
I went to blow the fire aflame,
But something rustled on the floor,
And some one called me by my name:

It had become a glimmering girl
With apple blossom in her hair
Who called me by my name and ran
And faded through the brightening air.

Though I am old with wandering
Through hollow lands and hilly lands,
I will find out where she has gone,
And kiss her lips and take her hands;
And walk among long dappled grass,
And pluck till time and times are done
The silver apples of the moon,
The golden apples of the sun.

W.B. Yeats

I will arise and go now, and go to Innisfree,
And a small cabin build there, of clay and wattles made:
Nine bean-rows will I have there, a hive for the honeybee,
And live alone in the bee-loud glade.

And I shall have some peace there, for peace comes dropping slow,
Dropping from the veils of the morning to where the cricket sings;
There midnight's all a glimmer, and noon a purple glow,
And evening full of the linnet's wings.

I will arise and go now, for always night and day
I hear lake water lapping with low sounds by the shore;
While I stand on the roadway, or on the pavements grey,
I hear it in the deep heart's core.

W.B. Yeats

My dear, my dear, I know
More than another
What makes your heart beat so;
Not even your own mother
Can know it as I know,
Who broke my heart for her
When the wild thought,
That she denies
And has forgot,
Set all her blood astir
And glittered in her eyes.

W.B. Yeats

The deep parts of my life pour onward,
as if the river shores were opening out.
It seems that things are more like me now,
that I can see farther into paintings.
I feel closer to what language can't reach.
With my senses, as with birds, I climb
into the windy heaven, out of the oak,
and in the ponds broken off from the sky
my feeling sinks, as if standing on fishes.

Rainer Maria Rilke

Never give all the heart, for love
Will hardly seem worth thinking of
To passionate women if it seem
Certain, and they never dream
That it fades out from kiss to kiss;
For everything that's lovely is
But a brief, dreamy, kind delight.
O never give the heart outright,
For they, for all smooth lips can say,
Have given their hearts up to the play.
And who could play it well enough
If deaf and dumb and blind with love?
He that made this knows all the cost,
For he gave all his heart and lost.

W.B. Yeats

When you are old and grey and full of sleep,
And nodding by the fire, take down this book,
And slowly read, and dream of the soft look
Your eyes had once, and of their shadows deep;

How many loved your moments of glad grace,
And loved your beauty with love false or true,
But one man loved the pilgrim soul in you,
And loved the sorrows of your changing face;

And bending down beside the glowing bars,
Murmur, a little sadly, how Love fled
And paced upon the mountains overhead
And hid his face amid a crowd of stars.

W.B. Yeats

THE PHOTOGRAPHS

Thanks to my wonderful family, Jayne, John, and Hannah; my mother, Frances; Joe Cunningham, Gary Chassman, Jill Bobrow, Dana Jinkins, Saul Winsten, Chuck Robinson, Tom and Barbara Harger, Beverly Penrod, Steven Niblo, and all the kind people of Madison County, Iowa.